A Whisper From God

by

Corliss Udoema

Copyright: 2025© (United States and International)

Copyright registered: USA Library of Congress Copyright Office: 03/25.

ISBN: 978-1948149235

Editor: Dawn Boyer, Ph.D., DBC Publishing
                           www.dboyerconsulting.com/publishingoptions

TABLE OF CONTENTS

To My Readers

As God has led me in writing each poem, may the words be a light and an inspiration to you. May you also be blessed to receive a special word from God.

The Lord has blessed me with a great and wonderful life. As I continue this journey, I desire to let my light so shine before men that they may see my good works and glorify my Father, who is in heaven. I pray continuously to always be a blessing to others as I share the love of God. May my life and poems be a living testimony of God's grace and mercy. May we remember our faith in He who set the captives free; know that because of the love that Jesus has for us, all things are possible. As a minister of God's word, I pray continually, without ceasing, for you.

May the Lord engulf you in His love and reveal His message in each of the poems. I pray you will always remember and reflect on how wonderful it is to be a child of the Most-High King.

If you are reading this book and do not know the Lord Jesus as your personal savior, Jesus is calling you to repent. Romans 10:9-10 says, 'If thou shall confess with thy mouth the Lord, Jesus, and shall believe in thine heart that God hath raised him from the dead thou shalt be saved.' For with the heart, man believeth unto righteousness; and with the mouth, confession is made unto salvation. Tell the Lord that you are a sinner and desire a place with Him in paradise. You can be a new creature in Christ, no longer bound in sin.'

Repeat the words of the sinner's prayer with your heart:

"Lord, I am a sinner. I confess with my mouth that I am a sinner and repent of my sins. I believe that Jesus died for me and that on the third day, He rose with all power in His hands. I believe that by the blood of Jesus, my sins are forgiven. Lord, I give my life to you. From this day forward, my life belongs to you, and I am no longer a sinner but saved by grace. I pray this prayer in Jesus' name. Amen."

If you have prayed this prayer, let me welcome you to the family of our Lord and Savior, Jesus Christ. Let the words herein be a pathway to higher peace, joy, and understanding.

Beloved in the Lord, may you be led deeper and deeper into His peace, His love, His grace, and His mercy.

I love you all in the name of Jesus.

With Love,

Corliss Udoema

Dedication & Acknowledgements

This book is dedicated to the memory of my late father, James 'Pediac' Pearson, and mother, Dorothy Bell (Dot) Pearson. Thank you for choosing me to be your child at the age of six months. You had all the choices in the world, but you chose me! Thank you. I shall always remember you!

To the memory of my late husband, Daniel Akan Udoema … you taught me your Yoruba culture, shared your love, and ultimately your name … 'Udo-ema' meaning … 'the one who is loved.'

My forever love for my spiritual father, the late Bishop Jesse Lee Williams, Sr. His anointing was awesome, and his gift for teaching the Bible was unmatched.

Once many years ago, I was having a problem with a manager at work and asked Bishop for advice. Bishop looked at me and simply said pray for him! My thought was, "Pray for him - pray for him?" Finally, I spoke and said, "But, Bishop, if I prayed for him, I wouldn't mean it." Bishop looked at me and responded, "Pray for him until you do mean it." My Bishop, a mighty man of God!

To the Rev. Dr. Gregory Nkrumah (Dr. K.), through good times and times of trials and challenges, you have been my wise and loving baby brother. I love how you preach the word, my brother, but more than that, I LOVE how you LIVE the word.

To my sister, whom God has healed and delivered from breast cancer, I love you. Reverend Rose McElrath-Slade, you are indeed an awesome warrior for the Lord. Your testimony is inspiring and encouraging. You will always be my sister in love.

To my Brothers in Christ who are around the throne of God, Rev. Otis Williams, Rev. Curtis Stewart, Deacon Morris Churchill, and Deacon Calvin Word – missing you always. Your legacy of love continues to shine in our hearts and in our lives.

To my Sisters in Christ, Deaconess Mattie Churchill, Nancy Speed, and Teresa Smallwood, you were healed on the other side of Jordan; we miss you and shall forever cherish your memory. Your legacy of love continues to shine in our hearts and in our lives.

Peace and blessings to our dedicated laborers in the gospel whom God has called and anointed as pastors: Rev. Wheeler Blount, Rev. Emmett Dunn, Rev. Dr. Augustus Henderson, Rev. Dr. Spencer Issac, Rev. Dr. Gregory Nkrumah K., Rev. Nelson Sneed, Rev. Dr. Gina Stewart, Rev. Dr. Cynthia Turner-Wood, Rev. Dr. Howard-John Wesley, Rev. Johnathan T. G. Wilkins, Sr., and Dr. Jessie T. Williams.

Fellow ministers in the gospel at Mount Olive Baptist Church, Centreville, Virginia, my church family at Mount Olive Baptist Church, Centerville, Virginia, and my church family at Mount Calvary Missionary Baptist, my home church in New Bern, North Carolina.

TRIBUTE PAGE

Love for My Daddy

From my first memories as a child, I knew that I was a daddy's girl. I loved my daddy, and my daddy loved me. My mother told me that even before I could walk, I would crawl over to the door about the time my daddy would come home for lunch or get off from work and wait for him to appear.

How did I know? Maybe it was my 'daddy radar' - LOL! Of course, I don't remember that, but it just made me realize that, even as a small baby, I loved my daddy.

I do remember one story. My daddy was getting ready to leave the house to go and visit friends at Mr. Gayre's place. This place was for men only, so Mama wasn't allowed to go, and as a little girl, neither was I.

However, I wanted to go with my daddy, and nothing he said would change my mind. He kept refusing, saying that I was too little and that it was too much of a walk for me. This didn't stop me from looking at him with my saddest face.

Even though my daddy knew that it was too long of a walk for such a little girl, I could feel him giving in the longer he looked at my sad face. He tried convincing me that he would take me somewhere later or give me a treat.

However, nothing my daddy said would make me change my mind. So, finally, off we went, walking from our home on Main Street to Mr. Gayre's gathering place for men (aka the 'shoe shine stand') in James City.

By the time we reached the bridge, I was so tired, but Daddy looked at me and said, "You wanted to come, so now come on."

Well, hot and tired, I walked the James City bridge that day! By the time we arrived, I was exhausted! It seemed we had only been there a few minutes when Daddy said come on, it's time to go home.

I never said a word, but as we approached the bridge, I looked at my daddy, and my daddy looked at me. I was so tired. As I thought about walking across that bridge, my eyes filled with tears, and they rolled down my face.

Daddy looked at me, reached down, picked me up, and carried me across the bridge. As you can imagine, that was my last time following my daddy when he visited Mr. Gayre!

Many years ago, my daddy transitioned to heaven, but there is never a day that I don't feel grateful for his love. This is a bit of history of me walking the bridge, but most of all, it is me remembering my love for my daddy and my daddy's love for me!

Sunset

If we live long enough, the sunset of our lives we
must face
It becomes obvious in so many ways, that we don't
have long to run the race

In this season, it's not the fancy things,
that are beautifully wrapped and sent our way
It is rather the love of family and friends,
that we long to be blessed with each and every day

In our latter days, the people who are there to
brighten our day and give a helping hand
Are God's angels on assignment following His words,
if you love me, then love others, which is the greatest
command

I pray, Lord, that I redeem the time and bless
someone every day
Encourage my soul, Lord, with a burden to help
others no matter what may come my way

Now, there are more years behind me than those
that lie ahead
And "it is winter," so I must work while it is still day
because there are so many that must be fed

My life has changed so much over the years
It has been a mixture of happiness, joy and tears

Yet I don't live in regret but rather,
appreciate each day and lesson learned
Because I know that my life is a gift from God,
and is nothing that I earned!

John 9:4 (KJV)

[4] *I must work the works of him that sent me, while it
is day: the night cometh, when no man can work.*

God Delivers

When I think about God and who he is to me,
The one who, with miracle power, parted the Red
Sea

The people fled from pharaoh,
to escape the death of their firstborn
There was nothing else they could do,
so they ran to keep their hearts from being torn

All of a sudden, they looked,
and there was no more dry land
Confused, they looked at God and said,
where can we go, Lord? We don't understand

God smiled and said, "I didn't bring you this far to
leave you"
Don't believe me, just watch and see the miracle that
I will do

I am your God that created heaven and earth,
and put stars in the sky
Get ready to walk because the water you see now,
will turn to land that is dry

As soon as you reach safety on the other side,
You will be free from the enemy and no longer have
to hide

Please rehearse and remember,
that I have made you a strong nation
Always Know that I am your God,
who made all creation.

Exodus 14:21-22 (KJV)

[21] And Moses stretched out his hand over the sea, and the LORD caused the sea to go back by a strong east wind all that night and made the sea dry land, and the waters were divided.

[22] And the children of Israel went into the midst of the sea upon the dry ground: and the waters were a wall unto them on their right hand, and on their left.

A True Missionary

I am a missionary on the Battlefield for God
With the gospel of peace my feet are now shod
Determined to tell a hurting world that God is not
dead
Filled to the overflow because I know there are
many that must be fed

Whether I have a little or whether I have a lot
I never have to worry because I know God will
always bless what I've got
When I see someone that needs a helping hand
It is my mission to pray Lord help me to do the best
that I can

Praise God for Jesus and the hungry 5,000 that he
fed
There was only two fish and five loaves of bread
Instead of focusing on what we don't have or thinking
there is nothing we can do
Remember the miracles of Jesus and know that He
can always bring us through

We may have troubles and challenges that sometimes get us down
No worry just remember that in the end Jesus is waiting for us with our eternal crown
You can't block me or stop me from walking the Kings Highway
I am determined to make it no matter what may come my way

I'm strong in the Lord and the power of his might
He has given all of us the Armor to win this fight
You and I must daily spread the good news and His Word we must teach
Don't let time slip away because there are many souls that we must reach!

Isaiah 6:8-10 (KJV)

[8] *Also I heard the voice of the Lord, saying, Whom shall I send, and who will go for us? Then said I, Here am I; send me.*
[9] *And he said, Go, and tell this people, Hear ye indeed, but understand not; and see ye indeed, but perceive not.*
[10] *Make the heart of this people fat, and make their ears heavy, and shut their eyes; lest they see with their eyes, and hear with their ears, and understand with their heart, and convert, and be healed.*

So, Sow!

I prayed to God and told him of my need
He lovingly said, "My child
all you have to do
is sow a seed"

Sow a seed in faith,
with the greatest expectation
Know that I am Alpha and Omega,
I gave life to all creation

I see the look on your face,
when you have little in your hand
Have you forgotten how many times I carried you,
and there was only one set of footprints in the sand

Everything you need, not only I can,
but I will provide
I am always here for you...
under my wings, you shall abide

Continue to sow my child, and
always expect something great
Although the vision may tarry
remember, I'm your father, and I am never late!

Kings 17:7-9 (KJV)

[7] And it came to pass after a while, that the brook dried up, because there had been no rain in the land.

[8] And the word of the Lord came unto him, saying,

[9] Arise, get thee to Zarephath, which belongeth to Zidon, and dwell there: behold, I have commanded a widow woman there to sustain thee.

He Came

Away in a manger,
our Lord Jesus was laid to sleep
Born to be our Redeemer,
with God's love and power
our souls He would keep

He came to save us from death because of sin
Had it not been for Jesus
our new life, we would not
have been able to begin

He died on the cross
for the whole world to see
Now we can sing praises,
because of Him, we have the victory

As we celebrate the day that our King of Kings
was born to set us free
Let us shout glory hallelujah and never forget
that God sent Him for you and for me!

Hebrews 2:9 (KJV)

[9] *But we see Jesus, who was made a little lower than the angels for the suffering of death, crowned with glory and honour; that he by the grace of God should taste death for every man.*

Praising Our God

We give you, God, the highest praise
First, because You sent your son to die
But from the grave
you did raise

Second, no matter the problems
in life that come our way
By victory in Jesus, you bless us
with a "hallelujah praise your name" day

Finally, in you God, we trust
even in things that we cannot see
We give you thanks for saving us
and setting the captives free!

Psalm 34:1-4 (KJV)

[1] I will bless the Lord at all times: his praise shall continually be in my mouth.
[2] My soul shall make her boast in the Lord: the humble shall hear thereof and be glad.
[3] O magnify the Lord with me and let us exalt his name together.
[4] I sought the Lord, and he heard me and delivered me from all my fears.

Still Standing

When all seems like it is hopeless
Even though we have fought the good fight of faith
The road ahead looks dim
And it seems impossible to finish the race

Because of you, Lord, we are still standing

When troubles surround us on every side
And life has handed us a bitter pill
Tired, yet every day, we press on
Because we are always determined to do your will

Because of you, Lord, we are still standing

We have more month than we have money
It is a struggle to make ends meet
We pray and wait for an answer
Sometimes, we feel hope giving way to defeat

Because of you, Lord, we are still standing

We have tried and tried
Not to fall short of the goal
We do the best that we can
Knowing you are the keeper of our soul

Because of you, Lord, we ARE still standing!

1 Peter 2:2 (KJV)

[2] *As newborn babes desire the sincere milk of the word, that ye may grow thereby.*

Jesus is Alive

Come on, all of you Christians
stop hiding under the bed
I thought you told me that Jesus was alive
so why are you acting as if He is dead

I know that Jesus is alive and still
Keeping you and me
In the midst of the impossible, Jesus will show up
and perform miracles for the world to see

Our lives are filled with so much that is hard
yet we know not to fear
Because no matter the situation or where we are,
Jesus is always near!

Isaiah 41:10-11 (KJV)

[10] *Fear thou not; for I am with thee: be not dismayed; for I am thy God: I will strengthen thee; yea, I will help thee; yea, I will uphold thee with the right hand of my righteousness.*
[11] *Behold, all they that were incensed against thee shall be ashamed and confounded: they shall be as nothing, and they that strive with thee shall perish.*

Still

I thank you, Lord, for the heart
that you have given me
In spite of physical challenges
and the handicap that others may see

In this season of pain and so many things
that I am not able to do
I love you, Lord, and continue to stand
as your soldier, always trusting in you

Sometimes, in brief moments
when I start to have doubt
I remember that you have called me
to share what your love is all about

You said it's not enough to have
love in our hearts for our fellow man
We must also lend to the least of them
a helping hand

You said be not weary in well doing
for in due season we shall reap
But to receive those blessings,
we must not faint, and your word we must keep

I am a living testimony that you are a keeper
and that I am covered by your loving grace
Joyfully, I remember that one day, in the end,
I will see you face-to-face

You continue to use me, Lord, and show me ways
that I can bless my fellow man
You remind me with each breath
that you only hold me accountable to do what I can

I may not come in a fancy package,
and I may appear a bit worn
Others may look at me and see that it has been
many years since I was born

I am still holding on to my faith
and your love I will always share
Letting He that has an ear know
no matter the situation, you always care

God, I thank you in the name of Jesus
that you continue to use me in your plan
I promise to never take your shed blood for granted
and to always do what I can!

1 Peter 3:8-12 (KJV)

8 Finally, be ye all of one mind, having compassion one of another, love as brethren, be pitiful, be courteous:
9 Not rendering evil for evil, or railing for railing: but contrariwise blessing; knowing that ye are thereunto called, that ye should inherit a blessing.
10 For he that will love life, and see good days, let him refrain his tongue from evil, and his lips that they speak no guile:
11 Let him eschew evil, and do good; let him seek peace, and ensue it.
12 For the eyes of the Lord are over the righteous, and his ears are open unto their prayers: but the face of the Lord is against them that do evil.

You Don't See Me

I look and see you coming my way
Will you not see me again today?

Or, will you stop and say, "Good morning to you!"
I am praying that today, you will do something new

You are close, so I smile, but you put your head down
Your face is now covered with a familiar frown

I silently cry out, please, I need you to see me
Look closely; you see the man that I used to be

I truly understand how you can so easily pass me by
When I remember how I treated the homeless, it makes me want to cry

I never saw them as my sisters and my brothers
I was mean and hurtful as I turned up my nose on others

Looking at me, you would never know that I was
once like you
A family, a nice home, a great job, a busy life with so
many things to do

I never thought that something like this would ever
happen to me
My eyes were wide open, yet the disaster of being
homeless I did not see

I could go on and on about my breakdown and how I
tried but could not stop the fall
I could tell you how hard I struggled to keep going,
yet it was like I hit a brick wall

One by one, family and friends walked away; they
saw me as a broken shell
I had hit rock bottom, nowhere to go, and my
wonderful life was now a living hell

Weeks turned to months, and months turned to years
All my joy and happiness were now filled with
sadness and tears

I thought all hope was gone, but then I remembered the rock
I remembered His promise that I would always be a part of the flock

Like Job, what I had was restored, and I have even more
Because I got the courage to knock on the door

Inside, Jesus was waiting, to pardon all my sin
Step-by-step walking in faith, my new journey was about to begin

You don't see me ….no, you don't see the person that I am
You see the outside yet not realize I've been washed by the Blood of the Lamb

You see, I am forever changed, forgiven, made whole and set apart
Now, daily I am praying, that God will change YOUR heart!

Matthew 25:34-40 (KJV)

[34] *Then shall the King say unto them on his right hand, Come, ye blessed of my Father, inherit the kingdom prepared for you from the foundation of the world:*
[35] *For I was an hungred, and ye gave me meat: I was thirsty, and ye gave me drink: I was a stranger, and ye took me in:*
[36] *Naked, and ye clothed me: I was sick, and ye visited me: I was in prison, and ye came unto me.*
[37] *Then shall the righteous answer him, saying, Lord, when saw we thee an hungred, and fed thee? Or thirsty, and gave thee drink?*
[38] *When saw we thee a stranger, and took thee in? or naked, and clothed thee?*
[39] *Or when saw we thee sick, or in prison, and came unto thee?*
[40] *And the King shall answer and say unto them, Verily I say unto you, Inasmuch as ye have done it unto one of the least of these my brethren, ye have done it unto me.*

Watching

The Coronavirus has come spreading sickness,
and everyone is asking why
No one seems to understand this deadly disease,
and why so many people have to die

Millions are affected in the US …and
even more all over the world
It attacks all races, creeds, old, young …
it doesn't matter if it is a boy or girl

We are told to social distance
even loved ones cannot be near
Daily, we pray although so many of us
continue walking in fear

Churches are coming together,
saying we must pray
Yet many members are struggling,
just to make it day-to-day

Why is it happening,
and when will it end?
The weight of this pandemic is so heavy
our backs are about to bend

Unemployment has spiked,
and checks are nowhere in sight
It is now dark with despair,
and people are desperately looking for light

We see long lines of those in need,
looking for something to eat
Trying to hold on to hope,
struggling not to give in to defeat

I look at what is happening,
in places near and far away
I pray, Lord, have mercy;
please let us see a brighter day

After pouring out my heart
to God in prayer
I found comfort in the assurance
that I am always in His care

But I still hear people talking about
the virus here and worldwide
Death taking one and leaving another,
yet they were standing side by side

Folks are wearing masks, washing hands,
and standing six feet apart
Yet death continues its rage,
leaving behind those with a broken heart

Why is it happening,
and when will it end?
Are you listening, Lord?
I thought you were my friend

The Lord said yes, I am your friend,
who sticks closer than a brother
I am always with you, and
my love for you is like no other

Stop thinking about the situation –
the how, the what, the when, and the why
Don't forget that I loved you so much
I was willing to die

I died on the cross, but on the third day,
I got up from the grave
I rose with all power;
a promise to mankind that I would save

The price has been paid in full
over two thousand years ago
Remember, I'm on the right hand of the Father,
watching over ALL of you below

1 Samuel 9:16 (KJV)

[16] *'Tomorrow about this time I will send thee a man out of the land of Benjamin, and thou shalt anoint him to be captain over my people Israel, that he may save my people out of the hand of the Philistines: for I have looked upon my people, because their cry is come unto me.'*

Louisiana After the Storm

First came the rain, and destruction covered the land
Recovery became a sign that help was something
not really in the plan

So many people came and gave a speech or two
Shaking hands, hugging babies, yet in the end, there
was nothing new

There were many donations that never reached
those in need
The reason? Some kept the money, because of their
greed

From days to weeks, and even months to years
The struggle continued in spite of weariness and
tears.

US citizens were called refugees, in the land of the
free and the home of the brave
Yet, for every sacrifice that could be given …the folks
of Louisiana still gave

Hope gave way to reality in the passing of time
Yet the eyes of the world could not see the pain,
because they were still blind

By faith in God, the people of Louisiana returned to
rebuild on what remained
They returned … praying, hoping, standing on God's
promises, in spite of their pain

All the people that came to help with the recovery
have now gone their way
The people of Louisiana continue in faith because
God has promised a brighter day

Instead of water … oil came and caused new pain
Wounds not yet healed were open for all to see the
stain

The lights of the news crews were shining, on the
new story of the day
But, like in the past, they would quickly go away

What can be done, and more importantly, what can
we do
Prayer is always in order, but there is more required
of you

Remember, we are called to love in word … and in deed
We have prayed, but now we must seek, ways to supply a need!

1 John 3:18-19 (KJV)

18 My little children, let us not love in word, neither in tongue; but in deed and in truth.
19 And hereby we know that we are of the truth and shall assure our hearts before him.

Closed Door

I truly thank God that He saw where I was headed
and closed the door
I had high expectations where I was going, but the
door that He opened there was so much more

When I saw my door closing, I was filled with
sadness and dismay
Not knowing that what God had for me was so much
better in every way

The pathway that we choose may seem sunny and
bright
But just stop and think for a moment, God's way is
always right

As a child of God, we can always celebrate that
which we do not see
Let's be thankful for the precious promises that He
has given to you and to me

James 1:17 (KJV)

[17] Every good gift and every perfect gift is from above, and cometh down from the Father of lights, with whom is no variableness, neither shadow of turning.

Why Not Now…Why Not You?

Have you thought about all the pain that we see in the world today?
The hurting, the hungry, and the lost struggling so hard but not finding their way.

What if there was an open door…a pathway to free them from their pain?
What if there was something that you could do and in the process, joy you would gain?

Just stop and think for a moment when we see something, how hard we pray.
Yet we do not extend a helping hand because we think - what difference would it make anyway?

Don't stop praying because truly in our prayers there is power.
Just don't forget to get up and do something because now is the hour.

To say that we have love is not enough to help heal what is broken.
Our actions are needed now, not words that do nothing to help when they are spoken.

My question today is, why not now, and why not you?
God needs our love in action because there is great work that we must do!

Matthew 14:13-21 (KJV)

¹³ *When Jesus heard of it, he departed thence by ship into a desert place apart: and when the people had heard thereof, they followed him on foot out of the cities.*

¹⁴ *And Jesus went forth, and saw a great multitude, and was moved with compassion toward them, and he healed their sick.*

¹⁵ *And when it was evening, his disciples came to him, saying, This is a desert place, and the time is now past; send the multitude away, that they may go into the villages, and buy themselves victuals.*

¹⁶ *But Jesus said unto them, They need not depart; give ye them to eat.*

¹⁷ *And they say unto him, We have here but five loaves, and two fishes.*

¹⁸ *He said, Bring them hither to me.*

¹⁹ *And he commanded the multitude to sit down on the grass, and took the five loaves, and the two fishes, and looking up to heaven, he blessed, and brake, and gave the loaves to his disciples, and the disciples to the multitude.*

[20] *And they did all eat, and were filled: and they took up of the fragments that remained twelve baskets full.*
[21] *And they that had eaten were about five thousand men, beside women and children.*

Your Hands

What if Jesus came and said,
"Show me your hands"
Would He see evidence of labor
or broken promises and unfulfilled plans

We say that we love Him and promise
to love our fellow man
But in our day-to-day living,
we seem to forget to follow this command

We identify ourselves as a child
of the most-high King
But our sacrifice of praise
we do not bring

The words that we speak
fall on deaf ears
Because faith without works,
no one hears

Jesus wants us to open our hands
so He can see the scars from our labor
It is what we do for others
that brings about true favor

So let us pray, then get up
and give someone a helping hand
Remember, you're not alone; just look down,
and you will see HIS footprints in the sand!

Psalm 41 King James Version (KJV)

*Blessed is he that considereth the poor: the Lord will
deliver him in time of trouble.*
*The Lord will preserve him and keep him alive; and
he shall be blessed upon the earth: and thou wilt not
deliver him unto the will of his enemies.*
*The Lord will strengthen him upon the bed of
languishing: thou wilt make all his bed in his
sickness.*

ENCORE

The following poems are included in this book for several reasons.

Over the years since publishing my first book in December of 2016, I have heard from many of you by phone, LinkedIn, Facebook, email, and text. Thank you for your support and encouragement to keep going.

When I finally decided to release the words and thoughts God had shared with me over the years, I could not believe I had put the release on hold for over twenty years!

Are you wondering why?

Although God had spoken each word to me, I felt that I wasn't enough because I had never attended seminary or had a degree in religious studies.

Every time I thought of myself releasing a book, I would immediately imagine someone picking up my book and quickly putting it down after reading the section about the author!

I knew God had spoken the words to me because I never started by writing a few lines and then putting them aside until I could think of something else to add. Each of the poems, no matter how long or how short, was written from beginning-to-end in one sitting because God gave me every word. Sometimes, I was not even given the name of the poem until the end!

I remember there was a time when a very dear brother in the Lord passed, Reverend Otis Williams, and I wanted to write a poem in his honor. I never told anyone of my hope to write the poem for fear that I would not be able to do it.

That turned out to be a good thing because the day of the funeral arrived, and I had only a blank piece of paper. No words, no title, nothing! After I returned home, I went to my bedroom, sat on my bed, and God spoke each word to me with the title ... "You Showed US."

Several years after publishing my first book, I am back to share words God has spoken to me. As I reread poems from my first book, I decided to select several of the poems so many of you had reached out and shared how they positively inspired you.

I am blessed to share with you several poems from my first book that are included in a special section of this book. This section has been named Encore. An encore is a repeated, or additional, performance at the end of a concert … as called for by the audience. Not only are you my audience, you are my friends, and you are my family.

So, as you read the poems in the Encore section, I pray that some of your favorites are among those included. My prayer is that as you read the poems in this book that, you – like me – will hear God's voice.

Inspiration for *You Showed Us*

This poem is dedicated to the memory of the late Reverend Otis Williams and his legacy of love. Reverend Otis Williams was a wonderful, loving, and caring man. As I think about him now, I can hear him saying, "How are you doing 'darling?'" It made me feel special, but then again, that was Reverend Williams.

He had a way of making everyone feel special and loved! Though we all knew that he called *all* the women' darling,' we always greeted him back with a smile and walked away feeling special. One of the most beautiful things about it was everyone, and I mean everyone, knew there was only one 'heartbeat of love' for Reverend Williams, and that was his beloved wife, Deaconess Tina.

As he came in and out of our lives based on his assignments from God, we were sad to see him go and rejoicing to see him return. During the last months of his life, we watched as he bravely and lovingly continued to work for the Lord.

He could be counted on to be there. He could be counted on to greet you with a smile. If he was not having a good day, we certainly didn't know it. Oh, how we loved him, and we were truly blessed because he loved us back.

On the evening after his funeral, I sat on the side of my bed. As I sat there thinking about my wonderful friend, words began to flow like the tears that washed my face. I was hurting, I was crying, and yet I found myself smiling as I scribbled the words about my friend, Reverend Otis Williams.

Be blessed as you read about my friend whom God called from labor to reward ...

You Showed Us.

You Showed Us

You showed us that
it is for God we must live
You showed us by example
to give the best that we have to give

You showed us how to climb mountains
with a smile on our face
You showed us that it is important
not only to run but to finish the race

You showed us how to be faithful
over what we do for the master
You showed us how to keep moving forward
even in the face of disaster

You showed us how to always treat
everyone with love
You showed us how to set our affections
on things above

You showed us how to be faithful
in what we do and say
You showed us how to cherish
each other in every way

You showed us the meaning
of how a real soldier must stand
You showed us how to live God's word
and take possession of the land

You showed us how to fight the good fight
even when your health failed
You showed us that you were battlefield-ready,
you would not be derailed

You showed us commitment to Christ
and determination to stand
You showed us there is a Lily in the Valley
and you were holding His hand

You showed us how to sing with joy
even near the close of the day
You showed us how to keep moving,
never losing sight of the straight and narrow way

You showed us how to see the sunshine
in the midst of a stormy sky
You showed us how to have a joyful melody
even when it was time to say goodbye

You showed us how to live
And, yes, you even showed us how to die
You showed us how to accept it all
never asking why

You showed us that you lived your life
according to the master plan
You showed us, my brother
That you were God's man.

2 Timothy 4:7 (KJV)

[7] … have fought a good fight, I have finished my course, I have kept the faith:

My Inspiration for:
The Prayer of the Perfect Christian

I was on my way to church one Sunday when suddenly, I heard a loud noise coming from the rear of my car. I pulled over quickly and stepped out of the car. I saw my left rear tire had blown and was completely flat. I stood there praying, asking the Lord to come to my rescue. I was alone and did not know how to change a tire, nor did I have a cell phone to call for help.

As I stood there praying, I looked up just in time to see one of the deacons from my church and his family approaching on their way to morning service. They looked at me, and I looked at them. In disbelief, I watched as they quickly drove right past me. Ok. I said the devil is a liar, and I will not let him steal my joy.

Seconds later, I saw one of our choir members approaching. Again, he looked at me and I looked at him, but this time I was dumbfounded as he also quickly kept going right past my disabled car.

At this point, I am talking to the Lord. Lord, you know I am here alone. You said in your words that two are better than one because they have a better reward for their labor, but woe to the one who is alone because if he falls, there is no one to pick him up. Lord, you know that I am a widow and a widow indeed. You promised you would be my company keeper and my provider.

At this point, the unexpected happened. A police car stopped, but instead of offering to help me, they were getting ready to write me a ticket. Apparently, I was parked in the wrong place. Ok. This was not going to end nicely.

I opened my mouth in praise and prayer and told those young men I was on my way to church. I said I could not help but stop because my rear tire blew out. I needed someone to help me fix my tire, or I needed a ride to church.

Well, you know God can put the heart of the king in your hands. That said, he put the heart of those young officers in my hands, because they assisted me in getting my tire changed and did not give me a ticket.

Remember the deacon and the choir member? I was later told that both of them mentioned to several people in the congregation they saw me on the side of the road. But, they neglected to share they had passed me by, leaving me there alone.

After this experience, I began to think about 'religious folks' that 'major' in tradition and 'minor' in relationship with Jesus. Oh, the perfect Christian, they are truly busy with their own perfection while they diligently check off the boxes in preparation for their heaven-bound experience.

They also have to devote time to get the beam out of the eyes of others. They feel compelled to share the sermon that brings correction to the lives of others. They are very quick to pray for the faults of others. As model Christians, they must stay up on their pedestal, lest they rub elbows with those who have not arrived at their level of Christian perfection.

These folks are so 'religious' and upright that they delight in correcting the preacher, training the deacons, coaching the trustees, directing the missionaries, expounding on the Bible study lessons, bringing reformation to the Sunday school class, and, of course, giving the Lord some tips on how to handle folks who are not meeting the 'Christian' standards.

Mercy me! They are so busy I wonder if they will have time to make it to Heaven! This poem is dedicated to *Perfect Christians* all over the world.

The Prayer of the Perfect Christian

Jesus, you won't believe
what happened to me today
I was minding my own business
In my everyday Christian way

When out of nowhere
Came this old drunk
He was so dirty
He smelled worse than a skunk

I pinched my nose
To block out the smell
But he had the nerve to speak to me
And say I'm doing very well

Can you believe
he stopped to talk to me
Doesn't he know I'm your child
A light for the world to see

Every day, they come
The drunks, the needy, and the poor
I can't believe they keep coming
As many times as I've slammed my door

So, Jesus, this is my prayer
and please put it in first place
You see, I'm so sick and tired
Of this whole human race

I want more
good upstanding Christians like myself
Ones who are not begging
But have some financial wealth

Jesus, please remove from my path
Those who can hardly read and write
When I have to be around them
I can't help but notice they're really not too bright

How can they do
What they can't possibly understand
It's the ignorant folks I'm talking about
The ones who can't even spell command

I'll be so glad
When I get up to heaven with you
Away from all these folks
Who make me feel like beating them black and blue

Jesus, I hope you didn't miss
Good old cousin Sally
That was last Saturday night
She got drunk and fell down in the alley

She's no good
And will never cause you anything but a frown
I guess everybody knows
She's run after almost every man in town

Now, Jesus, it's those types of people
I'm talking about
But I don't want to forget those crazy ones
That do the Holy Ghost shout

I tell you, they're always carrying on
such a ruckus and a fuss
If I weren't on my way to heaven
it would be enough to make me cuss

You see what I have to live with
And this is all the time
The drunks, the crazies
And the ones begging for a dime

It seems that every time
I'm on my way to church for worship and praise
Someone has the nerve to ask for my help
These nuts must be in a daze

Oh, for the day
That I'll get my reward from you
It's got to be a lot
With all that I've been through

I won't hold You
Cause these folks need a lot of working on

Jesus?
… Jesus?
… Hmm
I think He's gone!

Luke 18:9-14 (KJV)

[9] And he spake this parable unto certain which trusted in themselves that they were righteous, and despised others:

[10] Two men went up into the temple to pray; the one a Pharisee, and the other a publican.

[11] The Pharisee stood and prayed thus with himself: God, I thank thee, that I am not as other men are, extortioners, unjust, adulterers, or even as this publican.

[12] I fast twice in the week, I give tithes of all that I possess.

[13] And the publican, standing afar off, would not lift up so much as his eyes unto heaven, but smote upon his breast, saying, God be merciful to me a sinner.

[14] I tell you, this man went down to his house justified rather than the other: for every one that exalteth himself shall be abased, and he that humbleth himself shall be exalted.

My Inspiration for: Thank You, Jesus

Years ago, I heard the late Reverend Otis Turnage, of Mount Zion Holiness Church in New Bern, North Carolina, preach about having the Word in our heads, our hearts, and our hands. For years, I had the word in my hand and my head. I could easily open the Bible and quickly find scriptures to read. As time passed, I was also able to remember many of the scriptures.

What was missing was the power of having the word in my heart. So, are you wondering what is the difference? The difference is that God is all about the heart. The Bible says that the Lord searches the heart and tries the reins to give every man according to his ways and according to the fruit of his doings.

The Lord does not search our hands or our minds, only our hearts. It is having the word hidden in our hearts that lets us conquer instead of being conquered. It is having the word hidden in our hearts that lets us love and not hate our enemies.

It is with a grateful heart I shall never forget what Jesus did for me. It is with a grateful heart I shall never forget how He set me free. It is with a grateful heart I will always remember to thank the Lord for saving me.

For me, He suffered, bled, died, and rose from the dead so that we might have a chance for eternal life.

This poem is dedicated to all those who one day laid down in defeat, but thanks to Him who is able to keep us from falling … they rose up in victory.

Thank You, Jesus

Thank you, Jesus
for doing a new work in me
Thank you, Jesus, for the fire
burning so bright in me

When I first met You
I knew at a glance
That without You in my life
I didn't stand a chance

Over the rough roads of life
and down the valley of despair
There was no hope left
and no one to care

On pillows soaked with tears
and a heart that was broken
When I heard your sweet voice, Jesus
I knew You had spoken

The world offered its best
but I was still full of pain
And Satan had me bound
with the strongest chain

But in a brief moment
You touched my wounded heart
And I found myself saying
"Satan, from me, you must depart"

You started working
on filling me up with Your love
Then You told me to
set my affections on things above

You told me You had
prepared a place for me
You said in My name
from Satan, you are forever free

You told me of the victory
and the blood that You shed for me
Oh, thank you Jesus
for the new life You have given me

You placed in my heart
my head and my hand
The message of salvation
for the unsaved man

And just when I thought
Your work was complete
You told me how to bring
the enemy down in defeat

I started out a sinner
with no hope in sight
When I looked again, Jesus
I was on the battlefield to fight

In one hand was the sword of the spirit
the precious word of God
I looked at my feet
they were now Holy Ghost shod

I had the shield of faith
and the helmet of salvation on my head
Oh, thank you, Jesus, that over the enemy
I have the power to tread

Jesus, how can I thank You
for opening my blind eyes to see
Oh, I know, I can live
so that others can see You in me.

Ephesians 6:12-13 (KJV)

[12] *For we wrestle not against flesh and blood, but against principalities, against powers, against the rulers of the darkness of this world, against spiritual wickedness in high places.*
[13] *Wherefore take unto you the whole armor of God, that ye may be able to withstand in the evil day, and having done all, to stand.*

My Inspiration for: Leading with Love

Nehemiah is the ultimate example of leadership. As a former civilian working for the United States Navy, I was blessed with many leadership opportunities. I participated in many training and leadership classes; however, my greatest example of true leadership is found in the book of Nehemiah.

When Nehemiah heard the news that his people were in trouble, he went to the king and asked for permission to leave so he could help them. Upon arriving at his destination, Nehemiah quietly and prayerfully went out at night to assess the situation. After doing so, Nehemiah called the people together to do a work for the Lord. He did not focus on what skills the people had nor the sad state of the materials he had to use.

Nehemiah only focused on the work God needed them to do. I call that a faith experience.

After organizing the people and establishing a plan for the rebuilding efforts, Nehemiah had what I call a commitment experience. Nehemiah would not stop moving forward to accomplish his appointed task. He could not be frightened, he could not be enticed, he could not be lured, nor could he be discouraged. I call that a steadfast experience.

Today, there are Nehemiah's in our midst. Sometimes, you might meet him at church, at work, at a gas station, at a sporting event, or even standing in line at a grocery store. Late one night, I met a Nehemiah in the lobby of a hotel.

It was after one of the evening sessions of the General Baptist State Convention of North Carolina. I shared a room with two other ladies, and we had managed to do everything that evening except have dinner. At about 10:00 o'clock that evening, I was tasked to pick up our delivery order from a nearby restaurant in the downstairs lobby.

Because it was late at night, and I was only to be downstairs for a few minutes to pick up the delivery order, I didn't bother to change from my 'in the room clothes.' So, with a bandana on my head, a faded tee shirt, and what we in North Carolina call 'knee knockers' and flip-flops, I made my way down to the lobby. I stood at the desk and waited. Forty-five minutes passed, and no food. One hour and three phone calls later, still no food. My roommates were begging me to wait for the order because they were starving, and so was I. It was now almost midnight, and – you guessed it – no food.

I heard voices and saw several association members, one of which I instantly recognized. Of course, they saw me because there was nowhere to hide. I was truly embarrassed. We exchanged greetings, and the gentleman I recognized asked me, "What was I doing in the lobby by myself so late at night?"

Because of my appearance, he probably thought I was accidentally locked out of my room. I told him I was waiting for our food to be delivered. He asked how long I had been waiting, and I responded, "About two hours." He said, "Don't wait any longer; we have plenty of food in our suite; we are on the way out; just go up to the suite and tell them I sent you."

I graciously thanked him and watched them walk away. I was thinking … 'No way am I going to someone's suite looking like this.' He must have read my thoughts because he suddenly stopped and turned around. Seeing that I had not moved, he came back and said, "Come on, I will walk you up to the suite."

So, Nehemiah, the leader, Nehemiah, the caring and compassionate man of God, Nehemiah, the anointed servant, stopped to help someone he didn't know. I call him Nehemiah, but the one that stopped that night was the Rev. Dr. Gregory Nkrumah K. (Dr. K.), who at that time was the newly elected President of the General Baptist State Convention of North Carolina (a membership of 1,600 churches) and pastor of St. Paul's Missionary Baptist Church, Charlotte, North Carolina. (Under his leadership, the church grew by more than 3,500 members to over 6,000 members, of which more than half had come by baptism.)

Dr. K would also later be elected and serve as the national president of the Lott Carey Foreign Mission Convention, which partners with indigenous communities and leaders around the world.

To the least of them, let us receive them with the love Christ Jesus placed in our hearts. May the peace of God rule in our hearts. I pray you are blessed as you read *Leading with Love*.

The poem is dedicated to my friend and brother in Christ, Dr. K. My brother, you said, "I understand the difference between authority and power." Yes, you do; you built trusted relationships; the hurting, the hungry, the broken, and the lost filled the house and heard the message of salvation.

Bless you, for your tireless quest to spread the gospel inside and outside the walls.

Leading with Love

I am the leader
Who is leading with love
The agape kind
From the Father above

When you lead with love
You have a different approach
You realize it's your responsibility
To encourage and coach

Leading by example
Instead of do as I say
With the Holy Spirit leading
And guiding you along the way

I ask and do not demand
For a job to be done
Laboring in love
The obstacles are easily overcome

Your errors I won't discuss
In idle conversation
I'll teach you so we can benefit
From your full participation

I cannot be you
Nor can you be me
But we are called to be a light
For the world to see

For God is love
And Jesus gave us a command
As he loved us
We are to love our fellow man

Oh, it's easy to say that we love
Our sister and our brother
But it's hard to see, by the way
We sometimes treat each other

I've learned that it's not what you can give
But what you can take
I've learned that it's so easy
To magnify someone else's mistakes

I've learned to look at you
Through eyes of love
I've learned not to focus on me or you
But the Father above

I cover your transgressions
And put them in the past
I hold fast to love because
It's the only thing that will last.

Nehemiah 2:18 (KLV)

18 Then I told them of the hand of my God which was good upon me; as also the king's words that he had spoken unto me. And they said, let us rise up and build. So, they strengthened their hands for this good work.

Inspiration for: I See Too Many

I sit quietly and listen to words that pierce my heart. I watch as the tears well up in his eyes as my friend tells me his story of a broken relationship. Not with his wife, not with his children, not with a family member or a friend, but with his church. If this were the first time I had heard the story, it would be different.

Sadly, it is a story that I have heard too many times over the years. I have heard the story from church members, non-members, deacons, ushers, trustees, and, yes, even preachers. The locations and the names are different, but the stories are the same … hurt and wounded inside the church.

How does this happen, and what do we do about it? How can we, as loving ambassadors of Christ, stop the chain of hurt that prevents us from accomplishing our true, meaningful, and purpose-driven mission – which is spreading the good news of Jesus Christ?

How do we get to the place in Jesus where His love is overflowing in our lives? How do we get to the place where His love in us draws others to Him? How do we get to the place where we feel the hurt and pain of our brother and sister when no words are spoken? How do we get to that place where we have and take time to help each other? How do we get to that place where our thoughts are loving, our hugs are comforting, and our words are encouraging?

Maybe, just maybe, if we would have the loving heart of Christ to simply love each other, not for who we are, but *whose* we are; love will overflow, and change in the church will happen.

This poem is dedicated to all those with hearts overflowing with love.

I See Too Many

I see too many hurting, and too many broken
I see the look … no words have to be spoken

I see too much loneliness, and too much despair
I see too many faces that tell me, that there is no one
to care

I see too many sad eyes, welled up with tears
I see too many pressed down by doubts and fears

I see too many shut out, for one reason or another
I see too many longing for the comfort of a sister or a
brother

I see too many walking out, the same way that they
came in
I see too many overcome by the battle they feel they
can't win

I see too many tired of waiting for a broken heart to
mend
I see too many that are in need of a kind and
encouraging word from a friend

I see too many!

I see you!

I see me!

1 Peter 3:8-9 (KJV)

*8 Finally, be ye all of one mind, having compassion
one of another, love as brethren, be pitiful, be
courteous:*
*9 Not rendering evil for evil, or railing for railing: but
contrariwise blessing; knowing that ye are thereunto
called, that ye should inherit a blessing.*

My Inspiration for: A Man

He is the kind of man you will find praying and studying the word of God. You know him as a man whose steps are ordered by God.

His family respects him for being a Godly man. He takes on the nature of Nehemiah as the leader of his family. He shows leadership in his church and his community. He has the faith of Abraham, believing that when God says, 'He is able to perform it.' He takes on the courage of David, because he knows it is not what is in his hands that gives him the victory, but whose hands he is in.

He has the determination of Jacob, saying, "God, I won't let go until you bless me." He has the 'waiting' power of Moses, knowing 40 years is not too long to wait to do the work God has called him to do! Mighty men of God, hold fast to your faith and be blessed as you read *A Man*.

This poem is dedicated to the late Bishop Jessie Williams, pastor and teacher … in the 'church without walls,' and my granddaddy, the late Deacon Ossie Andrews.

A Man

A man of honor
And a man of goodness I long to be
When I look in the mirror
A man of truth and justice I pray to see

A man who builds bridges of understanding
And seeks to make peace in every way
A man who, in love, serves as head of his household
Each and every day

A man who loves God
With his soul, heart, and mind
A man who for God's sake
Is gentle, meek and kind

A man who knows that all he is
And ever hopes to be
Is what God whispers in his ear
As he bows down on bended knee

A man who presses for the prize
And never gives up the fight
A man whose steps are ordered by God
Determined to do what is right

A man who fasts and prays
Because this is God's command
A man who leans not to his own ways
Because he knows it is on God's promises
That he must stand

A man who God has given authority
Over the air, sea, and land
A man who is not afraid
To humble himself before God's almighty hand

A man who never ceases to praise God
And bless His Holy Name
A man who openly cries out to his father
Tears flow, yet he has no shame

A man who knows that what he sows
He shall also reap
A man that knows it is not his plan
But the masters that he must keep

A man who is found faithful
At the beginning and ending of each day
A man who never forgets to thank God
For just one more chance to pray.

Corinthians 15:58 (KJV)

Therefore, my beloved brethren, be ye steadfast, unmovable, always abounding in the work of the Lord, forasmuch as ye know that your labor is not in vain in the Lord.

My Inspiration for: A Woman

The woman is a neighbor who always opens her heart and doors to the needy. You can easily recognize her as the woman who always freely gives to others. She is a faithful woman of God who is always there with a heart full of love and compassion for others.

Who is this remarkable woman of God?

I am sure you know her. Maybe you call her Mom, mother, mama, or mommy. Perhaps her name is Grandma, Granny, Gammy, Mama, Big Mama, GG, Mamaw, Nana, or Nona. She could be called wife, sis, auntie, or cousin.

The woman could be called Anna. She is the mighty woman of prayer who never tired of being in His presence. The woman who sat outside the gates but who knew her place was wherever Jesus was.

The woman could be called Esther. She was a woman who was determined to seek an audience with the King. A woman of courage and direction who went covered with prayer and fasting and stated, "If I perish, I perish, I am going to see the king."

The woman could be called Ruth. She was a woman of loyalty and faithfulness whose alliance and allegiance was not based on situations or circumstances. She was a woman who tirelessly gleaned in the hot sun to bring food for her family. She was the woman who lovingly stood by her mother-in-law despite Naomi's situation.

The woman may be nameless like the woman from Samaria, the Shulamite woman, the woman with the issue of blood, or the widow. Or, the woman may YOU.

Be blessed as you read *A Woman*.

This poem is dedicated to Brenda Carradine, Co-pastor of International Harvest Christian Fellowship Church and author of 'Lady Preacher.' Carradine is a mighty woman of God who is tireless in her efforts to preach the word.

A Woman

A woman of honor
And a woman of grace I long to be
 When I look in the mirror
A woman of love and kindness I pray to see

A woman who shares with others
And has an encouraging word to say
A woman who will work
While it is still day

A woman who fears God
And always seeks His favor
A woman who never tires
Of doing God's labor

A woman who goes to the well
In the heat of the day
A woman who clings to Jesus
And remembers to watch, as well as pray

A woman who joyfully shares
What salvation is all about
A woman who touches the hearts of many
And trusts God without doubt

A woman who stretches out
Her hands to those in need
A woman who will always reap
Because she knows the value of one seed!

Proverbs 31:20 (KJV)

[20] *She stretcheth out her hand to the poor; yea, she reacheth forth her hands to the needy.*

My Inspiration for: My Greatest Love

I had no idea how special the day would be for Barbara that bright, sunny day I walked into her office. However, the moment I saw tears streaming down her face, I knew Barbara was a broken woman. In my heart, I realized Barbara was having a 'Leah experience' and she was feeling unloved, unwanted, and unappreciated. When you have been there yourself, it is easy to read the signs of an aching heart, shattered dreams, and broken promises.

Over several years, I had the occasion to share many things with Barbara, but today, I knew the Lord was knocking on the door of her heart. It was her appointed time to respond to the Lord's call. Barbara needed true love. Barbara needed a love that would stand the test of time. Barbara needed unconditional love. Barbara needed the love that only our Lord and Savior, Jesus Christ, can give.

I began to share the love of our Lord and Savior, Jesus Christ, and the resurrection power of His blood; Barbara began to cry. I spoke with

Barbara of an old rugged cross, an early morning rising, and Jesus ascending into heaven to sit on the right hand of God.

Barbara began to say in between sobbing, "I have been in a relationship with someone outside of the bonds of matrimony for 25 years. Even now, I am not sure I can break the ties." Barbara looked at me and asked, "Why would Jesus save me?" I simply responded, "Because He loves you, Barbara. Jesus is waiting with open arms. It is never too late to receive the gift of salvation."

The Bible says to come as you are and let the power of the blood shed by Jesus cleanse you from all unrighteousness. I told Barbara to come as the woman with her back bent with a spirit of infirmity for eighteen years.

Come as the woman of Samaria who went to the well in the heat of the day. Come as the woman with the issue of blood for 12 years who touched the hem of His garment. Come as the beloved in the Lord and receive salvation by the Lord's grace and mercy.

That day, Barbara gave her life to the Lord. As we embraced and cried tears of joy, I told her, "You have given your life to the Lord; you are now a new creature in Christ."

Later that night, I began to think of who I was before I was saved by the blood of the Lamb. As I thought about how far God had brought me. I began to thank Him for allowing me to lead another soul to Him. Oh, love, sweet love, my greatest love … Barbara had now quenched her thirst with water from the well of life.

This poem is dedicated to every woman who has felt or feels unloved, unwanted, or unappreciated. I invite you to come, taste, and see that the Lord IS good. He will be your greatest love.

My Greatest Love

When I look back over my life
And what I've been through
I realize that what has kept me
Was the love of Jesus so sweet and so true

I haven't always been
What God called me to be
Yet, I knew in my heart
That He still loved me

Sometimes, it wasn't easy
When people judged me
And said that I didn't measure up
They told me I wasn't even worthy
To drink from God's Holy cup

But I cried out in a loud voice
Like the man who was blind
I held on to grace
And remembered that mercy was still mine

I said, Jesus, I've been searching
And never finding what's missing in my life
I'm tired of the pain
the loneliness and the strife

I'm tired of wearing a smile
To cover the pain that I feel inside
I'm so ashamed of my life
But I know I can no longer hide

God reached out
And gently took my hand
And begin to share the gospel
And His redemption plan

God said it is my desire
That all will come and receive
All you need, my child
Is the faith to believe

I listened to the plan of salvation
As my eyes filled with tears
Because I realized that is what
I had been longing for so many years

Praise God that I received Jesus
As my Lord and Savior, that day
Now, I am depending on Him
To lead me and show me the way

I am a new creature in Christ
And began life anew
Now I have my greatest love
And that love Jesus is You!

Isaiah 54:4-8 (KJV)

[4] *Fear not; for thou shalt not be ashamed: neither be thou confounded; for thou shalt not be put to shame: for thou shalt forget the shame of thy youth, and shalt not remember the reproach of thy widowhood any more.*

[5] *For thy Maker is thine husband; the Lord of hosts is his name; and thy Redeemer the Holy One of Israel; The God of the whole earth shall he be called.*

[6] *For the Lord hath called thee as a woman forsaken and grieved in spirit, and a wife of youth, when thou wast refused, saith thy God.*

[7] *For a small moment have I forsaken thee; but with great mercies will I gather thee.*

[8] *In a little wrath I hid my face from thee for a moment; but with everlasting kindness will I have mercy on thee, saith the Lord thy Redeemer.*

My Inspiration for: The Ring on My Hand

For years, I was a very religious person.
I had been in church all my life and knew all the Bible
stories. But, something happened in my life that
caused me to crumble emotionally. The once happy
and outgoing person I was - disappeared. I became
a sad, sobbing recluse. This happened when I lost
my earthly father, whom I loved, cherished, and
adored. I had been a daddy's girl all my life.

I remember the story my mother used to tell
me. She said when I was a baby, every day, just at
about the time my daddy would come home for lunch
or at the end of the workday, I would crawl over to
the door and start looking out. Even though I could
not tell time, something triggered inside me, and I
knew when to go to the door to watch for my daddy.

Over the years, my daddy was my friend, my
defender, the one I would talk to about my problems,
and the one who always made me feel better by
smiling and saying, "It will be all right, little girl." The
fact I was a grown woman didn't matter. I was still

daddy's little girl. Oh, how I loved my daddy. When my daddy passed, it seemed my whole world had collapsed. I was always strong, but I became weak, helpless, and hopeless.

In the middle of my sorrow, it seemed my heart was so broken I thought I would never stop hurting. However, something happened at the lowest point of my life. I found a true relationship with the Lord. I found comfort in His word, and His truth became my shield and protection. I found hope in His promises. I found joy even in my sorrow. I found love and peace. Yes, I found a friend and a comforter. Jesus gave me a ring … a most beautiful ring. He has one for you, too.

Read and be blessed as you read *The Ring on My Hand*.

This poem is dedicated to all those out there feeling that you've done too much, that you've gone too far, that you're down too low to come home … Jesus is waiting, and he has a ring just for you.

The Ring on My Hand

The ring on my hand
Is something to see
I was given by God's grace
And was nothing done by me

I was lost and alone
An enemy of God
With the gospel of peace
My feet were not shod

With tender, loving mercy
And love from His Son
He spoke to my heart
And told me the race could be won

I thought about my life
How empty and sad
But when I thought about Jesus
I became exceedingly glad

I remembered He laid down His life
So that I might live
God loved me so much
He gave the best that He had to give

The pain that He suffered
On Calvary that day
Let the world know He is the light
The truth and the way

The riches He offered
To even a sinner like me
The price of salvation
No charge; it's free

He is my rock
On Him I depend
No matter the battle
Jesus can defend

When He went to the Father
He didn't leave me alone
The comforter, the Holy Spirit
Now makes me His home

The ring on my hand
Is something to see
It was given by God's grace
And was nothing done by me

Eight jewels are on
My beautiful ring
Given to me by Jesus
The King of Kings

Peace, hope, patience
Are three of the stones
I'm so glad I'm flesh of His flesh
And bone of His bones

Access by faith
Experience and love
Three more of God's blessings
From above

Glory in tribulation
And joy are the last of the eight
Thank God for my salvation
And the fact that I didn't wait too late!

Luke 15:20-22 (King James Version)

[20] And he arose and came to his father. But when he was yet a great way off, his father saw him, and had compassion, and ran, and fell on his neck, and kissed him.

[21] And the son said unto him, Father, I have sinned against heaven, and in thy sight, and am no more worthy to be called thy son.

[22] But the father said to his servants, Bring forth the best robe, and put it on him; and put a ring on his hand, and shoes on his feet:

My Inspiration for: You Are

I sat on my balcony in Puerto Rico at 4:30 a.m. It was quiet, except for the sound of the water splashing against the rocks. It was peaceful and I was praying and thanking God for just being God.

I thought about my life and how God had brought me over the rough roads and dried my tears. I started to think about how He had provided for me. I thought about how He had healed me.

At that point, I thought about the fact God is so many things to me. I began to pray 'thank you' to The Lord, Most High, The Lord, The Everlasting God, The God Who is Sufficient for the Needs of His People, The Eternal Creator, The Lord our Provider, The Lord our Banner, The Lord our Healer, The Lord our Peace, The Lord our Righteousness, The Lord our Sanctifier, The Lord of Hosts, The Lord is Present, The Lord our Shepherd, The Lord our Maker, and The Lord our God.

You are … You are … You are …

This poem is dedicated to those who teach the word of God with wisdom and knowledge. They teach with a burden to share the gospel in such a way that ordinary people will gain an understanding of the Bible. They teach because their love of God compels them to lovingly share the gospel that Christ Jesus is our Lord and our Savior.

Special love to the late Bishop Jessie Williams, Rev. Dr. Larry Ponds, Sr., and Reverend Lawrence Gilmore.

You Are

You are my Hope
My joy and my rest
You are my wonderful counselor
My almighty God, by whom I am blessed

You are my Jehovah Jireh
And so much more to me
You are the miracle that came in the flesh
For all the world to see

You are my rock of ages, my crown of glory
The one who wipes away my tears
You are my Comforter, the Holy One
Who calms all of my fears

You are Abba Father, my Lord
Who reached out and saved my soul
You are my sweet Jesus
The King that I long to behold

You are my water
When I thirst in a dry place
You are my direction when I am lost
I close my eyes, and I see your face

You are my restoration,
The lifter up of my head
You are my blessed peace and quietness
Just like the Bible said

You are my burden bearer
And my ultimate healer
You are the eyes through which I see
Because you are my true revealer

You are my Balm of Gilead,
My brother and my friend
You are my Alpha and Omega
My beginning and my end

You are my breastplate of righteousness
And my strong tower
You are my help and my rock
You fill me with power

You are the Babe, the Christ child,
The horn of salvation
You are my precious and sweet Lord
The one who made all creation.

Exodus 3:14 (KJV)

[14] *And God said unto Moses, I AM THAT I AM: and he said, thus shalt thou say unto the children of Israel, I AM hath sent me unto you.*

About *Corliss A. Udoema*

Corliss Udoema, aka "365/24/7 Veteran Supporter' or "Mama U," is an innovative and results-oriented entrepreneur, philanthropist, evangelist, missionary, author, and international motivational speaker. Most of all, she loves the Lord and prays continuously for opportunities to lift the name of Jesus.

She is a lifelong community worker recognized for her contributions to assist and improve the quality of life of those in need. God has blessed Udoema to travel to fifty-nine countries and eight islands, where she ministered, encouraged, and shared the good news of Jesus.

Udoema is a twice-published author and a poet. Her most recent book, *Words of Wisdom: Mama U Speaks on Business and Life,* is a refreshing, pocket-sized collection of "earned and learned" wisdom. The stories and quotes of wisdom are based on life and her personal experiences but can apply to any situation in life. One hundred percent of the royalties from sales of her books go directly to supporting the homeless, families in need, veterans, military service programs, and other non-profit organizations.

After retiring in January 2006 from the Federal Government with 33 years of service in various executive positions, including contracting, grants, and procurement, Udoema (CEO, President) started her own international professional staffing and management services company, Contract Solutions, Inc., that supports federal clients.

Under her leadership, CSI grew from a seed of less than $50 to a multi-million-dollar company, with one of those contracts being a 5-year, 40-million-dollar contract. As a company that consistently delivers professional excellence, CSI has earned five awards from INC Magazine as one of the fastest-growing companies in the USA and has been recognized twice as one of the fastest-growing companies in the Commonwealth of Virginia.

The Washington Business Journal featured Udoema as a Small Business Philanthropist. Her company, CSI, has donated *over* one million dollars to philanthropic charities in the metro area since 2017. In addition to financial giving, CSI is recognized as a top small business in the metro area for volunteer hours, logging 4,000 hours in 2024.

Udoema is a lifelong community worker who has been recognized for her charitable contributions by the Washington Business Journal as a Small Business Philanthropist for eight consecutive years and one of Prince William Living's Phenomenal Women. Udoema's notable recognition in business and the community led to her being included in the Congressional Record; she has also been the recipient of two Congressional awards and a Virginia Governor's Award on Volunteerism and Community Service, recognized by the Small Business Administration as third runner up for the National Small Business Person of the Year Award and the Small Business Administration's Small Business Person of the Year in the Commonwealth of Virginia, the Good Neighbor Award by Fort Belvoir Army Base, and presented the Presidential Lifetime Achievement Award by President Joe Biden.

She was educated in the New Bern, North Carolina, public schools and attended the University of Maryland. In the church at an early age, she carried on the work of an evangelist and a missionary her entire life, and in October 2002, she accepted the call into the ministry. On July 13, 2003, Udoema started preaching at her home church in New Bern, North Carolina, Mount Calvary Missionary Baptist Church, where her former pastor, Dr. C. D. Bell, presided.

CHARITIES SUPPORTED

About Agape Love in Action (ALIA), Inc.

Udoema is President of Agape Love in Action, Inc. (ALIA), a 501(c)(3) non-profit organization which she founded in March 2015. She is a true visionary who founded and serves as President of ALIA. Udoema realized her lifelong dream – to have an organization that would spread the love of God by helping those in need. ALIA is a 365/24/7 veteran supporter engaged in notable volunteer outreach projects, including Business Battle Buddy, Hope In A Bag, Wisdom Meets Technology, ALIA Foodbank, and Reach 2 Feed.

The Hope In A Bag project started over 16 years ago when Udoema asked Thanksgiving dinner guests to bring something to donate to the homeless shelter in lieu of food dishes. Since the first 40 bags of goodies were donated, ALIA has provided thousands of homeless people with bags filled with snacks and hygiene items, such as socks, hats, gloves, and encouraging words. The Hope In A Bag project recently collaborated with the Jacksonville Jaguars, where staff and family members packed 800 bags of food items and personally delivered them to local homeless shelters in Jacksonville, Florida. Udoema is excited about future collaborative opportunities with the Washington Commanders, who have donated thousands of hats and water bottles to veterans and the homeless. ALIA has packed and distributed over 125,000 bags to the homeless over the past ten years.

ALIA Foodbank opened in November of 2021 and provides food to families and organizations in need on a monthly basis. Since 2022, under the Director, Rev. Richard Hardy (US Army Retired) and Deputy Director Armand Quattebaum (US Navy Retired), about 150,000 pounds of food has been donated to military families, financially struggling families, senior citizens, children, and the homeless. In 2023 and 2024, ALIA delivered 850 turkeys and side dishes to fill the Thanksgiving tables of enlisted personnel at Fort Belvoir and other military installations in the District of Columbia, Maryland, and Virginia, including Quantico and Joint Base Andrews. Service members have also been provided with household cleaning products and supplies. The Army, Navy, Air Force, and Marine Corps are participating service members.

Reach To Feed program provides needy families with meals, food, water, and hygiene items when finding a simple meal during a disaster becomes challenging. Reach 2 Feed provides families, communities, and organizations affected by disasters with meals and necessities, based on the simple idea that helping can be infectious when it travels by word-of-mouth. The Reach To Feed program aims to spread the word via exponential communications. Those in the program give to one family and tell two other individuals. The concept is simple yet effective – help one family and tell two individuals – a simple concept using word of mouth that works to bring people together to make a positive difference during a time of great need.

The **Wisdom Meets Technology** project provides free training classes for senior citizens with limited or no computer experience. The project also provides free computers to seniors based on documented and qualified financial needs. The class sizes are capped at a maximum of eight students to ensure optimum learning. More than 2,000 senior citizens have graduated from the training program with the ability to navigate the internet, communicate through email, and use word processing software.

Business Battle Buddy is ALIA's program to assist and support active-duty military and Veterans. It is not just words – but actions – to offer family support to active-duty military and veterans. Business Battle Buddy also mentors veteran-owned small businesses with hands-on business mentoring services. In 2025, Udoema launched a podcast to make business advice readily available to small business startups, especially those owned by veterans.

Hero Love Boxes was initiated during the COVID-19 pandemic when ALIA lost access to homeless shelters. ALIA shifted their care bag deliveries to first responders in five hospitals in five counties (Prince William, Arlington, Loudoun, Fauquier, and Fairfax). A team of elementary school children beautifully decorated boxes that were filled with snacks and cards with words of encouragement to put a smile on the faces of the heroes serving on the front line during the pandemic. A local bank still uses the decorated boxes to collect food for needy families.

For more, follow: http://agapeloveinaction.com/

Lott Carey Global
Christian Missional Community

The Mission of the Lott Carey Global Christian Missional Community extends the Christian witness worldwide. Through prayer partnership, financial support, and technical assistance, we come alongside Indigenous communities to support evangelism, compassion, empowerment, and advocacy ministries. Together, we are touching lives with transforming love.

For more, follow: http://lottcarey.org/

If you enjoyed reading this book – you will want to read Corliss Udoema's previous books:

A Guiding Light
https://www.amazon.com/Guiding-Light-Reflections-encouragement-instruction/dp/1939774292/

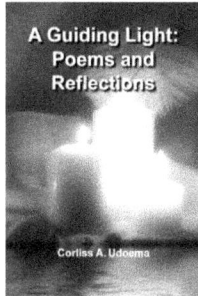

Words of Wisdom: Mama U Speaks on Business and Life

Print Edition
https://www.amazon.com/Words-Wisdom-Mama-Speaks-Business/dp/1948149206/

Kindle Edition
https://www.amazon.com/Words-Wisdom-Mama-Speaks-Business/dp/1948149206/

About the Book

Growing up in Eastern North Carolina and traveling to fifty-nine countries and eight islands, the author listened to God and, with loving obedience, wrote the words He spoke to her. It was surprising, yet clear, the words God spoke – were poetry. Poems were written on notebook paper, napkins, paper bags, and even torn cardboard boxes, but one thing was consistent about each writing: they all came as one complete thought.

Since the author published A Guiding Light: Poems and Reflections (2016), which was inspired by the Holy Spirit and Words of Wisdom, Mama U Speaks on Business and Life (2022), inspired by those who sought her business wisdom, she has continued to write as God has spoken.

Some of her poems are simple and short; they convey basic biblical principles. Other poems provide an instructional mini-sermon in an inspirational style.

From the beginning to the end, one thing is certain … you will hear God because you will hear His words. It will also be obvious that the author loves the Lord. In a warm, southern, conversational style reflective of her childhood in New Bern, North Carolina, the author opens her heart to share God's talks with her. She continues to be inspired by her walk of faith and lovingly shares a beautiful, inspirational book of poems.

www.ingramcontent.com/pod-product-compliance
Lightning Source LLC
LaVergne TN
LVHW051244080426
835513LV00016B/1729